Living with Little Quilts

Alice Berg
Mary Ellen Von Holt
Sylvia Johnson

Credits

Editor-in-Chief . . . . Kerry I. Smith

Technical Editor . . . . .Janet White

Managing Editor . . . . Judy Petry

Design Director . . . . .Cheryl Stevenson

Text and Cover Designer . . . . Amy Shayne

Design Assistant . . . . Marijane E. Figg

Copy Editor . . . . Liz McGehee

Proofreader . . . . Leslie Phillips

Illustrator . . . . Laurel Strand

Living with Little Quilts

© 1997 by Alice Berg, Mary Ellen Von Holt, and Sylvia Johnson

That Patchwork Place, Inc., PO Box 118, Bothell, WA 98041-0118 USA

Printed in Hong Kong
02 01 00 99 98 97   6 5 4 3 2 1

MISSION STATEMENT

We are dedicated to providing quality
products and service by working
together to inspire creativity and
to enrich the lives we touch.

Dedication

To the early quiltmakers who made the doll quilts we love so dearly and who inspired three friends to create the designs for Little Quilts. We also thank our families who have watched our collections grow and have only asked for one thing: a path to walk through the house!

Acknowledgments

The homes featured in this book belong to:

Wally & Alice Berg, Marietta, Georgia

Butch & Sylvia Johnson, Marietta, Georgia

Ron & Mary Ellen Von Holt, Marietta, Georgia

Charlie & Karin Snyder, Marietta, Georgia

Robert & Irene Barker, Dunwoody, Georgia

The photography (unless otherwise noted) is by:

Design and Visual Effects, Atlanta, Georgia

Dave Young, photographer

Some of the bears seen in the photographs are by:

North American Bear Co., Inc., Chicago, Illinois

Jody Battaglia, "beary best friends™," Marietta, Georgia

We would like to thank:

Susan Upchurch, computer consultant

Deborah M. Mix, editorial consultant

Library of Congress Cataloging-in-Publication Data

Berg, Alice,
    Living with little quilts / Alice Berg, Mary Ellen Von Holt, Sylvia Johnson.
       p. cm.
    ISBN 1-56477-192-X
    1. Patchwork—Patterns. 1. Quilting—Patterns. 3. Doll quilts.
    I. Von Holt, Mary Ellen,   . II. Johnson, Sylvia,   . III. Title.
    TT835.B377   1997
    746.46—dc21   97-16865
                                                                             CIP

Contents

What is it about these small textile treasures hanging so still on the wall or softly covering a tabletop? Why is the addition of a little quilt to your decor so special? To begin, let us tell you how we were inspired. Then we'll share with you ideas for collecting, sewing, and decorating with little quilts.

The Bicentennial year of 1976 restored interest in quilting in many ways. There were contests, patterns became available, and cotton fabrics were in demand as interest grew in this American craft. Books and magazines with photographs of charming country homes showed collections of antiques and cozy room settings. Quilts appeared everywhere: on a wall, on a table, draped over a chair, folded on a bench, and in other surprising places. Quilts added personality and friendliness to a room. The colors and pattern of a quilt made such a difference that it became hard to imagine decorating a room without some type of quilt.

For quiltmakers like us, that was an exciting time. As we dreamed through the pages of country decorating magazines, pretending we lived in those comfortable settings, we began to notice the presence of small quilts. They gave a softer look to a room

furnished with hard, primitive pieces. They added a bit of sweetness and whimsy. Hoping to create the feeling of some of the rooms we saw, we tried to purchase small quilts. We discovered that finding quilts like the ones we wanted wasn't easy, and if we did find them, they were usually expensive. We decided to make our own.

Even to experienced quiltmakers such as ourselves, making antique-looking doll quilts was not as easy as we expected. We wanted ours to look like well-used doll quilts from days gone by. The quilts we made looked too new. Eventually, after much experimentation, we managed to produce quilts with the look we wanted.

The three of us became obsessed with making doll quilts. The idea of selling them entered our minds, so we talked our way into a popular local antique show. We sewed nonstop and sold ninety-five little quilts in a few hours.

As time passed and we continued to sell the quilts, people began to collect them. Admirers who wanted to make their own began to ask for help, and this led to a pattern and kit business called Little Quilts™, with customers worldwide. Little quilts are easy to make, requiring simple supplies. They don't require stitching perfection—imperfect stitches can be part of their charm. Perhaps it's the feeling of connection with a time when the pace was slower that calms and delights us as we sew these little quilts and display them in our homes.

What Is a Little Quilt?

A little quilt is a small, but not miniature, quilt based on a traditional design, often used as a doll quilt. It is made just like a large quilt, consisting of quilt blocks, with borders, binding, and hand quilting. The pieces are easy to manage, and you can use various construction techniques.

This book includes six simple projects to make. Each is shown in a setting of our choosing. We hope you will use these patterns and projects to create special little quilts to use in settings of your own. If you are a beginner, you may need a little extra help from one of the many basic technique books available. For the experienced sewer or quilter, these projects are "dessert." Basic information about quiltmaking is in the "Little Quilt Primer" on pages 61–62.

Collecting

Most of us aren't lucky enough to own a collection of antique doll quilts, and the fact is they are hard to find. Today, quilters are making wonderful doll quilts using the many fabrics and patterns available to them. Fabric companies are reproducing favorite prints and designs from the turn of the century, and woven homespun fabric abounds. Newly made quilts resemble antique ones—with the right fabric choices. You can form a special collection of new doll quilts made by friends, family, or yourself.

You may want to collect old doll quilts for their look, or you may be more serious about your collecting. If you do plan to collect antique doll quilts, keep these points in mind. Depending on the purpose of your collecting, they may be important to you.

◆ Buy from a reputable dealer.

◆ Check the binding. If it appears too new, it might indicate that the piece was cut from an old quilt, and that there are several more just like it. If so, it is obviously not a true doll quilt and should be less expensive.

◆ Look at the backing fabric and quilting. It should be in keeping with the rest of the quilt and should not look new.

◆ Ask dealers for the history of a piece. Look for dates or initials on the quilt.

◆ Check the scale of the block. It should be small and in keeping with a doll-size bed.

Your purchase may not be of museum quality, but if it tugs at your heart, buy it. Remember, doll quilts are not perfect pieces. Little girls made them to play with and to learn how to sew.

Sewing

Here are some hints for making a little quilt:

◆ Make it like a regular quilt, but scale it down to a small size.
◆ Use fabrics on hand, slightly uncoordinated and scrappy.
◆ Use 100% cotton fabric.
◆ Choose small-scale prints, checks, and plaids.
◆ Use an accurate ¼"-wide seam allowance.
◆ Press often while you sew.
◆ Layer with **thin** quilt batting.
◆ Quilt simply, and tea-dye to produce an "aged" look.

When completed, press the quilt flat and let the decorating fun begin.

Tea-Dyeing Recipe

2 quarts hot tap water
6 to 8 tea bags

Pour hot water into a large bowl and add tea bags; steep 15 minutes. Remove tea bags. Add the finished quilt to the tea solution; soak 15 to 30 minutes. Rinse quilt in cool water. Lay flat to dry. Press to reshape.

Decorating

One of the wonderful things about a little quilt is that it can be used in so many ways: to decorate for a special occasion, to celebrate a season, or just as a pick-me-up in a certain place. Today, the little quilt looks great on the wall, but how would it look on a table or peeking out of a basket tomorrow? Subtle changes in decorating give your home vitality and make it special to family, friends, and most of all to you!

Treat yourself to a day of puttering around the house. While tending to the necessary chores a house routinely demands, rearrange little quilts and decorative accessories, finding new showplaces for them.

As you look at these pictures of little quilts used in so many ways, you will notice that some of the quilts, dolls, and collections are shown in more than one setting. A collection of wooden houses is perfect on the mantel, but it is also charming moved to the dining room table to make an interesting centerpiece.

What can you do with the collections you have? Do treasures go unnoticed? Are they scattered around in too many places? Use these tips for effective display in your home.

◆ Gather your complete collection of items and try to arrange them in one place.

◆ Look for items of the same color or theme to add to a collection. For example, add doll clothes, tea sets, valentines, and toys to a display of rag dolls.

◆ Arrange things in a whimsical way—as if someone had been there playing and just walked away.

◆ Choose a little quilt to complement the collection. Consider color or pattern. Imagine a Bear's Paw quilt with those silly old teddy bears!

◆ Decide where the quilt will be used—on the wall or under objects.

◆ Begin by arranging larger pieces and then fill in with all the smaller ones.

◆ Consider other related items to mix in.

◆ Use a small lamp as a spotlight, showing off colors and details.

◆ Look at the arrangement with a "crooked eye" to make sure everything is not lined up in a row—unless they are soldiers! Stand back, smile, and pat yourself on the back! Great job!

Hanging a little quilt on the wall is simple. A favorite way to do it is to pin two safety pins on the back and use them as hangers on small nails. Decorative hangers fastened to the top of the quilt are also effective. These may be purchased in quilt shops and through some catalogs.

Throughout this book, you will see a variety of ideas for using little quilts to decorate a home. Many of the accessories, such as dolls and folk-art pieces, are one of a kind, created by designers we admire. You probably have similar, well-loved objects to use as you create settings for your own little quilts. Your local quilt shop can provide books, patterns, fabrics, and classes for your every creative need. Try making a little quilt using one of the projects provided, and be on the "hunt" for authentic doll quilts at antique shops and sales.

Visit our book often, and each time something new will catch your eye—perhaps a wall arrangement or a quilt simply placed on a table. We all get ideas from each other, so choose the ones that fit your personality and lifestyle, and make your home a special place for those who live and visit there.

About the Authors

Mary Ellen Von Holt, Sylvia Johnson, and Alice Berg (left to right), have been designing and publishing patterns for Little Quilts™ since 1984. Living in Marietta, Georgia, they all enjoy collecting—especially quilts! As authors of **Little Quilts All Through the House** and **Celebrate! with Little Quilts,** they have shared their skills for making and living with little quilts.

On a Clothesline

A gathering of favorite dolls, toys, and little quilts cleverly displayed on a clothesline is ready for a summer tea party. What a lovely way to spend the afternoon! ❦

What do quilters and gardeners have in common? They both enjoy colorful designs—ones made with fabric and others with flowers. A child's picnic table and a wicker settee combine with little quilts and pillows in this garden setting.

"A yard…is like an extended living room." —Alice Walker

At the Door

How exciting to arrive at a friend's home with quilts, pumpkins, flowers, and friendly faces to invite you in! Decorating can begin outside your front door, even if only for a few hours. A pine cone heart on the brick walkway says "Welcome."

You can decorate foyers and powder rooms with a live-lier theme since guests are in those rooms for only a short time.

"Welcome to our home" describes this foyer perfectly. The red wallpaper provides a good background for a gallery of little quilts and their companions. A whimsical greeting awaits friends as they arrive.

WELCOME · FRIENDS

"The ornament of a house is the friends who frequent it."
—Ralph Waldo Emerson

It's obvious to arriving guests that a quilter lives here. It only takes one or two little quilts to create a friendly entrance.

"Not many sounds in life...exceed in interest a knock at the door." —Charles Lamb

A stairway makes a unique gallery for little quilts, which can be combined with other textures, such as pottery and baskets. This display will brighten many trips up and down. 🌸

By the Fire

A keeping-room fireplace is a natural gathering place for friends as well as collections. Centered over the mantel is an American flag behind an angel wreath. On each side is a red-white-and-blue little quilt—one antique and one new. Quilts also hang on a drying rack by the fireplace. A cozy rocker with pillows and a wool snowman make this the perfect place to be. 💜

Here, grouped items complement a fire screen covered with a Log Cabin, primitive-style hooked rug. Log cabin houses, a Log Cabin quilt, and greenery surround the screen, keeping the eye moving and adding interest. 🍃

Welcome

"There is no place more delightful than one's own fireside." — *Cicero*

Mantels are great locations for quilts and collections. Displays are easy to change, and they create a focal point for the whole room. Put out your favorite "happys!" ♥

In a Cupboard

Quilts with childlike themes go well with Raggedy Ann dolls, doll dresses, and wooden toys. Little quilts adorn cupboard doors, children's chairs, and toy boxes. Using red throughout the setting brings it all together. Imagine having all these smiling faces to keep you company!

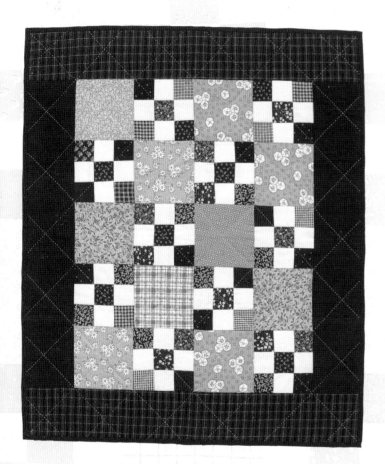

Rag Doll Quilt

Finished Size: 21½" x 25¼"

Make this little quilt for that special cradle that holds
your collection of rag dolls and old toys. Before
beginning, read the "Little Quilt Primer" on pages
61–62.

Materials: 42"-wide fabric

¼ yd. total assorted red prints
⅛ yd. muslin
⅓ yd. total assorted light green prints
⅓ yd. red border print or check
¾ yd. for backing
23" x 27" piece of thin batting
¼ yd. for binding

Directions

These measurements include ¼"-wide seam allowances.

1. Cut 50 squares, each 1¾" x 1¾", from the assorted red prints. Cut 40 squares, each 1¾" x 1¾", from the muslin. (Or use the strip-piecing method at right.)

2. Arrange squares of red and muslin into Nine Patch blocks and sew them together. Make 10 blocks.

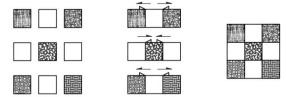

3. From the assorted light green prints, cut 10 squares, each 4¼" x 4¼".

4. Sew the Nine Patch blocks and green squares together in 5 rows of 4, then join the rows to make the quilt top.

5. Cut 2 border strips, each 3½" x 19¼", and sew to the sides. Cut 2 border strips, each 3½" x 21½", and sew to the top and bottom.

6. Layer the quilt top with the batting and backing.

7. Baste and quilt as desired. We suggest cross-hatched lines running through the blocks into the border.

8. Bind the quilt and add a label.

Strip-Pieced Nine Patch Blocks

Cut 1¾"-wide strips in random lengths from the muslin and assorted red prints. Sew the strips together as illustrated. Cut the segments 1¾" wide and sew them together into Nine Patch blocks.

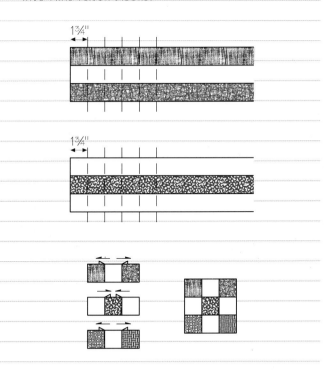

Cupboards are quaint, charming, and very useful. They come in all sizes, some with doors, and some without. Cupboards can go anywhere!

Several collections — flags, patriotic quilts, bears, and red-white-and-blue pillows — contribute to an Americana theme. ❦

Open cupboards provide a place to combine collections with little quilts of similar colors and designs. Baskets show off quilts and a pillow collection.

Cupboard doors and shelves offer another un-expected but perfect spot for more treasures.

A warm-hearted room says "Let's visit" by combining quilts, baskets, hooked rugs, lamps, and tin figures with country colors. A large room can hold several collections. An Americana theme is displayed on the wall above the sofa. Atop the cupboard between the two windows, a gardening theme reminds us to look outside.

"Rooms are like people. It takes time to get to know them, and even then, the interesting ones keep revealing themselves more and more." —Jane Stanton Hitchcock

On a Table

This sunny room holds a variety of treasures. Baskets, needlework, and quilts add texture and color.

Little pillows made from extra quilt blocks make great party favors.

Celebrate a friend's birthday with quilted pillows. Patchwork fabric is the wrapping, and raffia the ribbon. Placed in a basket, they become the centerpiece for the table. Hang a favorite quilt on the wall, light the candles, and sing "Happy Birthday."

"...the most charming hours of our life are all connected with a memory of the table." —Pierre-Charles Monselet

Tables are fun and easy places to use little quilts. Change them often to coordinate with celebrations. Flowers, baskets, and bowls would sit nicely on top to complete the centerpiece. Make sure your table always has a little quilt.

An antique doll quilt is right at home in this formal dining room.

A little quilt, in colors similar to the porcelain anniversary couple, enhances this setting.

"Thou shalt love and be loved by, forever..." —Robert Browning

In the Bedroom

ABC
DEFGH
IJKLM
NOPQR
STUVW
XYZ

SINGER

This crisp red-and-white bedroom is inspired by the patriotic eagle quilt. Framed prints, doll quilts, and collectibles in harmonizing colors complete the arrangement.

Amish rooms are simple and orderly. They are furnished with only useful and important belongings. Amish quilts are unique and often include intense colors—bright and pure—or grayed and muted tones. Solid fabrics, bold geometric designs, and fine quilting distinguish Amish quilts.

This bedroom blends Amish doll quilts with children's clothing and a hooked rug. The large primitive-style quilt on the wall acts as a backdrop. 🍂

Come into a cozy bedroom with full-size quilts, crib quilts, and little quilts. Two-colored quilts work best with the floral wallpaper. The well-dressed doll bed welcomes a guest. 🍃

Little Linens

Little linens, pillows, and mattresses for doll beds can be made from striped ticking fabric and antique linens found at flea markets and antique shows.

Mattress—Measure your doll bed, add ½" to each dimension, and cut 2 pieces of ticking fabric that size. With right sides together, join the 2 pieces of ticking fabric together on 3 sides, using a ¼"-wide seam allowance. Turn and stuff lightly with polyester fiberfill. Hand stitch the opening closed.

Pillow — Make a small rectangular pillow from homespun or ticking fabric. Sew and finish like the mattress.

Pillowcase—Cut 2 pieces of fabric 1" wider and 2" longer than the pillow. Sew the edges together on 3 sides. Finish the fourth side with a decorative border or trim as desired.

Another way to make an easy, elegant pillowcase is to fold an antique handkerchief in half. Leave the prettiest trimmed edge open and join the remaining 2 sides.

Sheet—Cut a piece of fabric 3" wider and 3" longer than the doll bed. Hem the edges on all sides.

Now you are ready to "make your bed."

Antique dresser scarves and doilies can provide trims for these sheets.

"Make me a child again
just for tonight!"
—Elizabeth Akers Allen

On the Wall

Noah's Ark is the theme for the dining room. Flying Geese, Log Cabin, and Star quilts are companions in this setting. Let's do lunch! 🐦

Turn-of-the-century Star blocks discovered at a flea market combine nicely with reproduction fabrics. Colors in the primitive Santa and animals blend well with the antique fabrics in the quilt.

Quilts are a respected form of American folk art, so why not combine them with other pieces? A colorful, scrappy little quilt is the focal point over a brightly painted table with a whimsical angel and a friendly wooden cat—notice the blackbird on the cat's tail!

Antique Star Doll Quilt

Finished Size: 12" x 16"

Antique quilt blocks suitable for reproducing doll quilts can be found at flea markets, antique shows, and garage sales. Blocks smaller than 6" are perfect for making little quilts. Before beginning, read the "Little Quilt Primer" on pages 61–62.

Measurements below are for making a quilt using 4½" blocks (unfinished size). Adjust the measurements and yardage requirements as needed to fit your blocks.

Materials: 42"-wide fabric

Six 4½" antique quilt blocks
¼ yd. for border
½ yd. for backing
14" x 18" piece of thin batting
⅛ yd. for binding

Directions

1. Press each quilt block and measure to determine which is the smallest block. Trim all blocks to the size of the smallest one. (It is all right if you must trim away some of the points. This adds to the charm of the doll quilt.)
2. Sew the blocks together in 3 rows of 2, then join the rows to make the quilt top.
3. Cut 2 border strips, each 2¼" x 12½", and sew to the sides. Cut 2 border strips, each 2¼" x 12", and sew to the top and bottom. Remember, if your blocks do not finish to 4", you will need to adjust the lengths of the border strips.

Not all little quilts need borders. Small Nine Patch blocks joined without borders make a great little quilt!

4. Layer the quilt top with the batting and backing.
5. Baste and quilt as desired. We suggest quilting along the seams of each star, and a single line down the border.
6. Bind the quilt and add a label.

Brighten your day in unexpected places! This master bath is accented with two little quilts chosen for their color. One hangs on a peg, and the other dresses up the vanity. 🖤

QUILTS

Little quilts, little pillows, and little treasures are fun to combine in a favorite spot. The wall between two windows is ideal for this small table and side chair. As you walk around the house, look for small spaces to warm up. 🖤

The corner of a room is unique because it offers two walls to work with. A hooked rug fits right under the shelf full of houses and bears. On the other wall are two antique doll-quilt reproductions. 🖤

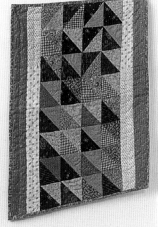

Sarah Jane's Doll Quilt

Finished Size: 17" x 20½"

This little quilt can be made to look like an antique doll quilt by combining assorted brown, pink, and black fabrics, and using light, medium, and dark shades of each color. If you use scraps of plaids and reproductions of antique shirting fabrics, your quilt will have a soft, charming look. Before beginning, read the "Little Quilt Primer" on pages 61–62.

Materials: 42"-wide fabric

Assorted small pieces of pink, brown, and black prints
⅛ yd. black-and-white print for border
⅛ yd. pink print for border
⅝ yd. for backing
18" x 22" piece of thin batting
⅛ yd. for binding

Directions

1. From the assorted pink, brown, and black prints, cut 32 squares, each 3⅜" x 3⅜", then cut them in half diagonally for a total of 64 half-square triangles.
2. Using a ¼"-wide seam allowance, randomly sew together dark and light triangle pieces to make 32 blocks.

For a fun hand-piecing project, make a plastic template of the triangle on this page and mark the sewing line on 64 small scraps of your favorite fabrics. Cut out the triangles, adding ¼"-wide seam allowances, and hand piece them together to make 32 blocks. This is a perfect carry-along project to work on in your spare time.

3. Sew the blocks together in 8 rows of 4, then join the rows to make the quilt top.
4. For the borders, cut 2 black-and-white print strips, each 2" x 20½", and 2 pink strips, each 2¼" x 20½". Sew 1 black-and-white strip and 1 pink strip to opposite sides of the quilt top.
5. Layer the quilt top with the batting and backing.
6. Baste and quilt as desired. We suggest hand quilting ¼" inside each half-square triangle block.
7. Bind the quilt and add a label.

Nothing is more exciting to a true collector than the "authentic piece." Here is a wonderful collection of antique doll quilts simply displayed. The personality of each quilt can be easily studied. Who made these quilts? Who played with them? ❀

'Tis the Season

Christmas is the ideal time of the year for decorating with little quilts, because they add color and warmth to walls and tables. The wooden village makes a special centerpiece on the Log Cabin quilt top. The colors from the table blend well with the folk-art appliqué crib quilt. Merry Christmas to everyone!

With bears, quilts, and marbles on the desk, it will be hard to put homework before play! ♥

Homework before play.

Crisp days and chilly nights—this fun corner is ready for anything from Halloween to an autumn harvest. These little quilts blend themes and colors to create a warm and comfortable setting. The masked bear with his jack-o-lantern is saying "Trick or Treat." ♥

"There is no season such delight can bring, as summer, autumn, winter, and the spring." —William Browne

One little quilt is all it takes to dress up this window area. A simple arrangement is often the best. ♥

Little quilts are just right for little spaces!

Christmas is a time to decorate all the nooks and crannies. Along with special plates in the plate rack and a wooden bowl filled with pine cones, greenery, and gingerbread men, holiday quilts welcome the season. ♥

Log Cabin Doll Quilt

Finished Size: 16½" x 20½"

The Log Cabin quilt block is always a favorite with quilters. This block is fun to make with strips of light and dark assorted fabrics sewn around a center square. Try using flannel fabrics for a special, soft little quilt that looks great anywhere. Before beginning, read the "Little Quilt Primer" on pages 61–62.

Materials: 42"-wide fabric

1 ¼"-wide strips of assorted colors in light and dark values
12 black squares, each 1 ½" x 1 ½"
¼ yd. for border
Scraps of fabric for appliqué pieces
Fusible web
¾ yd. for backing
18" x 22" piece of thin batting
¼ yd. for binding
Black or cream embroidery floss

Directions

1. To make a Log Cabin block, first sew a light strip to one side of a black square. Turn the block in a clockwise direction and add another light strip. Continue, sewing 2 dark strips, then 2 light strips to the block, ending with 2 dark strips as shown. Make 12 Log Cabin blocks.

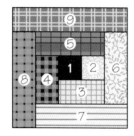

2. Sew the blocks together in 4 rows of 3, then join the rows to make the quilt top.
3. For the borders, cut 4 strips, each 2½" x 16½". Sew strips first to the sides, then to the top and bottom.
4. To appliqué flowers and leaves, trace the template patterns on this page onto fusible web. Following the manufacturer's instructions, iron the fusible web onto the flower and leaf fabrics. Cut out and iron the flowers to opposite corners of the quilt top.

5. Using 2 strands of black or cream embroidery floss, embellish the edges of the flowers with the buttonhole stitch (see page 62).
6. Layer the quilt top with the batting and backing.
7. Baste and quilt as desired. We suggest quilting through the center of each log and around the flowers and leaves. Embroidery floss or pearl cotton works well for quilting on flannel.
8. Bind the quilt and add a label.

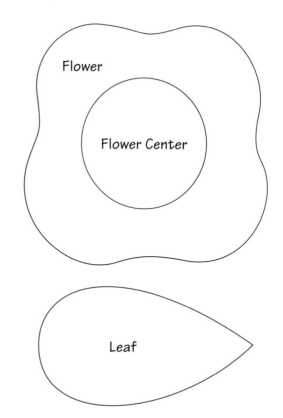

Flower

Flower Center

Leaf

Even the bears deserve their own tree, complete with a paper-doll garland. Little quilts on the wall and tabletop add color and whimsy to the teddy bear's Christmas. Santa bear is trying his best to make it down the chimney before the bears awake. 🐾

"I could live there" comes to mind while viewing this peaceful village. There is a cat for company, sheep for wool, and a home, school, and church. There is even a flag quilt for protection and a heavenly star quilt for warmth. ♥

Calico Stars Doll Quilt

Finished Size: 16½" x 19½"

This bright and cheerful star quilt is fun and easy to make, using small scraps of your favorite fabrics. Make this keepsake little quilt from those special fabrics you've been saving. Before beginning, read the "Little Quilt Primer" on pages 61–62.

Materials: 42"-wide fabric

⅓ yd. star print for background
Scraps of prints in assorted colors
Fusible web
¼ yd. for border
⅝ yd. for backing
18" x 21" piece of thin batting
⅛ yd. for binding
Black embroidery floss

Directions

1. Cut 20 squares, each 3½" x 3½", from the star print.
2. Trace 20 stars onto fusible web, using the template on this page. Following the manufacturer's instructions, iron the stars onto the wrong side of the assorted prints. Cut out the stars; press one onto each of the background squares.
3. Using 2 strands of black embroidery floss, embellish the edges of the stars with the buttonhole stitch (see page 62).

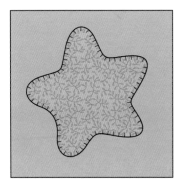

4. Sew the blocks together in 5 rows of 4, then join the rows to make the quilt top.
5. Cut 2 border strips, each 2½" x 15½", and sew them to the sides. Cut 2 border strips, each 2½" x 16½", and sew them to the top and bottom.
6. Layer the quilt top with the batting and backing.

7. Baste and quilt as desired. We suggest quilting around each star. Quilt wavy lines connecting the stars, and a wavy line in the border.
8. Bind the quilt and add a label.

Star

For the Bears

Bears have always been a part of Little Quilts™. Their faces are friendly and easy to work with. They are happy wherever we put them, and they never talk back!

This is a perfect spot for a bear family portrait—a church pew underneath a patriotic crib quilt.

In the 1800s, crib quilts were usually made for newborns by their grand-mothers and aunts because these women had the most quilting time. Pieced or appliquéd, these quilts were approximately 36" square. Quilters wanting to try a new pattern or tech-nique often found crib quilts to be a good size to work with. Some of these more elaborate quilts remain to-day because they were not used every day.

Recipe for charm: bears, little quilts, chairs, wooden toys, pillows, and books. Add one great wooden cupboard and arrange ingredients in a fun and loving way. Results: a charming cupboard with your favorite "goodies." ♥

Bees, bears, and honey! This powder room is full of surprises. ♥

As we grow older, we all look back fondly on our school days. Combining signature quilts, schoolhouse memorabilia, bears, flags, and flowers will help preserve memories of those golden-rule days. 💗

Everything works together: little quilts—both old and new—bears, pillows, hooked rugs, little linens, and accessories combine to create a warm and wonderful setting. 🍂

Follow the leader! Overall Bill is on his way to school. A small setting is created beneath a quilt near the fireplace. A flag, old school books, and children's toys complete the scene. 🍂

Remembering happy times...

In Special Places

Little quilts, finished or in progress, are inspirational in the sewing room. Dolls, rabbits, and a wool black cat provide companionship. Fabric neatly stacked in baskets and on shelves is both decorative and functional. 🐾

This rug-hooking area also serves as a place to display rugs and quilts. The snow-man appears in both wool and cotton.

"To be happy at home is the ultimate result of all ambition." —Samuel Johnson

Often one color can blend quilts and accessories together. In this setting, black predominates in the quilts, the doll chair, and sewing machine, and contrasts well with the red-and-cream checked wallpaper. Amish quilts, antique sewing tools, books, and dolls would delight any quilter. ♥

Come to the country for a quiet Sunday morning. The farmhouse quilt makes a good background for a mother and son on their way to church. On top of the dresser is an antique doll quilt. ♥

Little Quilt Primer

Rotary Cutting

You can use a rotary cutter, an acrylic ruler, and a mat to accurately cut several layers of fabric at one time. These tools, purchased at quilt shops and fabric stores, are invaluable for making multi-fabric quilts.

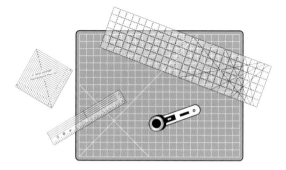

Machine Piecing

Use a ¼"-wide seam allowance. Often what we *think* is a ¼"-wide seam allowance is too wide or too narrow. Use a ruler or graph paper to check. Set the stitch length at 10 to 12 stitches to the inch, and use a neutral thread color. Since seams will cross each other, backstitching is unnecessary. Pattern pieces are shown actual size and do not include any seam allowance. Add ¼" around each piece.

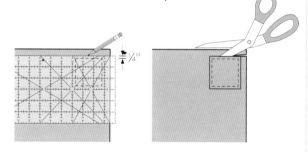

Hand Piecing

1. Make a template of each pattern piece. Transfer grain-line markings to your templates.
2. Place a template on the wrong side of the fabric, aligning the grain-line arrow with the grain of the fabric. Using a sharp pencil, trace around the template. The line you've drawn is the actual sewing line.
3. Add the seam allowance by cutting the piece out ¼" beyond the sewing line.
4. Pin pieces together, matching the seam lines. Sew on the lines, using a small running stitch. Sew only from one seam intersection to another so that seam allowances remain free. Trim seams to ⅛" after pieces are sewn together.

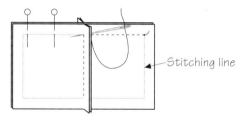

Stitching line

Buttonhole Stitch

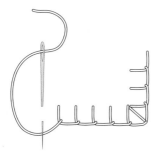

Quilting

Mark quilting lines lightly with an ordinary pencil, washable fabric marker, or white pencil. Cut backing fabric and quilt batting a few inches larger than the quilt top all the way around. Layer the backing, batting, and quilt top. Baste the layers together.

Quilt, using small, even stitches through all layers. Hide beginning and ending knots by pulling them gently through the quilt top into the batting.

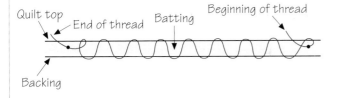

Binding

1. Trim away excess batting and backing fabric from the quilt.
2. Cut strips of fabric for the binding 1 ¼" wide across the width of the fabric. Sew together enough strips to go around the quilt plus 4" to 5".
3. Place the binding on the quilt top with right sides together and raw edges even. Sew through all layers, using a ¼"-wide seam allowance.
4. Stop stitching ¼" from the corner, backstitch, clip threads, and remove the quilt from the machine. Fold the binding up, then bring it down. Stitch from the edge as shown. Repeat at each corner.

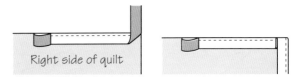

Right side of quilt

5. When you reach the starting point, sew the end across the beginning fold. Cut off excess binding. Bring the raw edge to the back of the quilt, fold under ¼", and blindstitch in place, covering the machine stitching.

Back of quilt

Resources

American Sampler
959 Canton Street
Roswell, GA 30075
(770) 993-1843

The Chandlery
950 Canton Street
Roswell, GA 30075
(770) 993-5962

City Art Works
2140 Peachtree Road NW
Atlanta, GA 30309
(404) 605-0786

Indiana's Antiques
3519 Broad Street
Chamblee, GA 30341
(770) 455-8357

Heart of Country Antique Show
(February)
Nashville, Tennessee

Lakewood Antiques Market
(2nd weekend of each month)
Atlanta, Georgia
(404) 622-4488

Pride of Dixie Antique Show
(4th weekend of each month)
Atlanta, Georgia

The following That Patchwork Place books offer complete information on basic quiltmaking techniques and more:
Little Quilts All Through the House
Celebrate! with Little Quilts

For catalog and mail-order information, send $2.00 to:
Little Quilts
4939 Lower Roswell Road, Suite 204C
Marietta, GA 30068

Selected Books from
That Patchwork Place

At Home with Quilts • *Nancy J. Martin*

Celebrate! with Little Quilts • *Alice Berg, Mary Ellen Von Holt & Sylvia Johnson*

Decorate with Quilts & Collections
• *Nancy J. Martin*

Little Quilts • *Alice Berg, Mary Ellen Von Holt & Sylvia Johnson*

Patchwork Pantry • *Suzette Halferty & Carol C. Porter*

Quilts Say It Best • *Eileen Westfall*

The Total Bedroom • *Donna Babylon*

These quilting books are available at quilt, craft, and book stores. Call 1-800-426-3126 for the name of the quilt shop nearest you.